PRA
LILY-

"'On Earth, a fish barricades her den / and emerges male two months later, / melon-head worthy of brawling and teeth,' announces one of the brilliant sectioned poems central to *Lily-livered*. 'On Mars, the sunset is blue. / She asks me about this second life / of red dirt, burnt skin. What do you enjoy // about being a man?' Although framed by a series of 'transiversaries,' to describe this collection in diaristic terms would not do justice to the overlay of questions raised around gender, beauty, diet, desire, violence, medication and self-medication. An interest in refrain and cyclical structures anchors us, pleasingly counterbalanced against enjambment and an adventuresome sense of the line; we welcome cultural cameos from Shakespeare, HBO, and indie rock. This is a stunning read that showcases a sophisticated, exciting approach to contemporary poetics."

— Sandra Beasley,
author of *Count the Waves*

"Cyclical and dreamy, yet sinewy, Wren Hanks' *Lily-livered* is a record of the hungers—for food, for sex, for alcohol—that simultaneously tie us to and alienate us from our bodies. Though a site of suffering and addiction, the physical in *Lily-livered* is also a conduit for pleasure, connection, and transformation, where 'a girl prayed let me be sea / and ended up a man.' *Lily-livered* portrays embodied living in all its ambivalent, bloody glory, while summoning the tenderness to 'cradle everyone I cannot save, myself included.' Hanks wakes us up to the sublime, precarious selves housed in these strange, disgusting, beautiful bodies—and you will feel more alive for having read it."

— Luiza Flynn-Goodlett,
author of *Look Alive*

"*Lily-livered* is a beautifully braided catalog of ways to live and not die. Wren Hanks writes on friendship, hunger, touch, transformation, and the inheritance of a trait for which the chapbook is named. 'Imagine it happened in a barn, a meat cellar.' These poems unfurl as an array of forms, forms of life, with sensuous patterns and particulars. With 'stubble the possible field,' Hanks breathes lines that combine ribaldry, romance, and refrain into stunning, surprising images and interconnections. This is a smart, moving collection that you will love reading alone or with friends. 'The ground is safe.'"

— Oliver Baez Bendorf,
author of *Advantages of Being Evergreen*

LILY-LIVERED

WREN HANKS

DRIFTWOOD
PRESS

Independently published by *Driftwood Press*
in the United States of America.

Managing Poetry Editor: Jerrod Schwarz
Cover Image: Denis Sarazhin
Cover Design: Sally Franckowiak
Interior Design & Copyeditor: James McNulty
Fonts: Caslon Book BE, Cinzel, Garamond,
Maecenas, & Merriweather

First published in March 2021
ISBN-13: 978-1-949065-10-7

Please visit our website at www.driftwoodpress.com
or email us at editor@driftwoodpress.net.

Contents

"Go, prick thy face, and over-red thy fear, Thou lily-livere'd boy."

—*Macbeth: Act 5, Scene 3*

Inheritance

My great-grandfather killed himself with a sawed-off shotgun.
Imagine it happened in a barn, a meat cellar

like the one in *Westworld* where Teddy's re-programmed
to be capable of violence. I've never seen a picture of him,

my great-grandfather, and wonder if he squinted
like my grandmother, who drowned herself

about a mile from my house. I haven't seen
a picture of myself where I look real yet, but I covet a body

I could hurt time and time again, *die to come back new.*
Imagine I tell therapists my ideation is passive, an inheritance

that won't let me discern a pig's shoulder from a gun.
Teddy gazes so fondly on the field swallowing him whole

he makes it to heaven, that same field re-programmed
toward benevolence. Imagine I can't tell a creek-bed

from a flooded river, whether I'm safe
inside one or the other.

TRANSIVERSARY

The further I get from being a woman the less I'm stared at while eating. Eggplant parm, fries dripping truffle oil, fries dripping cheese whiz, appetizers washed down with gulps of beer (never water). I'm not skinnier than I was pre-T, but I'm not fatter either. It's the difference of: maybe a chubby man is not the person you'll go home with tonight (or any night), but you accept his hunger as legitimate. When I was six years old, and legitimately overweight, belly rolls dripping over a plaid skirt (oh the rich kids who witnessed this, like a pencil being thrust through their 18-karat eyes), my friends threw away my Hostess cupcake and force-fed me a red delicious apple. When I was 31, my girlfriend baked me cookies and served them to me on her knees, told me she liked the solidness of my body in words too convincing to be false. Still, some of us lie well. I said *I feel sexy* when I meant *the apples in my belly come up my throat, bob with me in this rotten barrel.*

BARRICADES

On Mars, the sunset is blue,
polar, familiar, I could be its snow queen
with that audience of burned red dirt.

On Earth, a fish barricades her den
and emerges male two months later,
melon-head worthy of brawling and teeth.

Transition works this way for some,
but when I barricade myself it's to worry
the new hairs on my jawline until they fall out.

—

She asks me if I want to learn violence
the way men know it, the mare glue
setting them to the street.

I might ask you to strike me again and again,
not as a woman, but something to control.

Do you want that stoic brutality?

If I barricade myself, it's because the answer
became yes.

I took her leash and became her audience,
the view polar, familiar.

—

On Mars, the sunset is blue, my wife says.
I could be that body, ice-flushed, growing crystal.
But she wants to be the first person kicking its dust.

On Earth, I read to her about the matriarchal society
of spotted hyenas. I'm angry the researchers keep
referring to a female hyena's "pseudo-penis."

That's just her penis, I keep saying.
Like mine.

When I go on like this she barricades herself
in her office, cocooned from a body, mine,
she barely registers as familiar.

—

Twin Peak revisits the gas station
from my dreams where I barricade

myself from dead dive bar patrons,
knife-hands curled behind their backs
as they spill Wild Turkey on the cement.

The answer, for years now, has been
Nightmare a Night.

I pick wilting creatures off my bedroom floor.
I cradle everyone I cannot save, myself included.

—

On Mars, the sunset is blue.
I wake up with checkered fleece balled in my fist,
skin mites displaced by drool.

There's a cave shrimp that gets 21%
of its nutrients from methane.

There's a man who doesn't hide his breasts
beneath a binder when the exterminator comes.

If I barricade myself for the rest of the morning,
it's because the *ma'am's* became (always were) my fault.

Polar, familiar, a stare never aimed at my eyes.

—

A stare never aimed at my eyes:
she starts her story,
the one where she's shaking

a can of crispy onions against my ear.
The precipice of sex, she says.
A cliff you should seriously jump over.

Warm a girl up first? she teases
when I hit her with my wedding band on,
the barricades are mental. We're allowed this.

My body on ice most of the week.

—

On Mars, the sunset is blue.
She asks me about this second life
of red dirt, burnt skin. *What do you enjoy*

about being a man? How my clothes never come clean,
how I stink like a thawing mammoth sawed into.
The new science of me:

inflated muscles, the beer belly, the inability
to clone me now, exactly as this.

—

What do you enjoy about being a man?
Like the horror frog, I'll disconnect tissue,

when threatened. *What do you enjoy?*
Release the claw barricaded
in tissue. Release, snap the bones,

each sunset on earth with her
I ask if we're ready for violence yet.
Being a man, inhaling to pull

the claws back through my toes.
Release, *amphibian, snow queen,*
belie this polar ache.

TRANSIVERSARY

The further I get from being a woman the less they stare. I'm offered mole, extra rolls, drizzled cheesecake. I remember, at five, telling my mom I wanted a second hot dog in a pool of bread. I couldn't finish it, left ketchup under my nails and all over my purple dress, but she told me to finish what I'd asked for (*always finish what you've asked for*) so I choked and spit the hot dog up on my plate.

The further I get from being a woman this first Xmas on T, wearing my binder under pajamas, watching Michigan snow fall, hiding needles so my wife's parents won't think I'm on heroin. Her mother pours condensed milk into the broccoli casserole as my stomach curls into itself, an agitated fern leaf.

Why can't I show them my hairy stomach when they call me a girl? *Balk, if you must, at what you've asked for:* I'm not lying to your daughter.

TRANSIVERSARY

The further I get from being a woman I'm still not safe. Not from the man on the subway who spits in my face but, mostly, not from myself. I've started to repeat *Pain is Luminous Pain is Luminous* when I scroll through the news feed, when I skip lunch to reach a client on time, when another trans friend asks me what we're living for and there's no good answer.

Is there a good answer? the ideation, axolotl-cute and just as capable of breathing underwater, asks my maxed-out credit card. *Is there a good answer?*, my student loans, the top surgery out of reach. I know I'll never go without meds because my rich boyfriend has promised me so; as he orders us another plate of garlic bread, he says *please, just tell me what you need.*

L E G I B L E

I'm not legible to straight men, I say,
summer grass stain, sugar ant in the Plaza pantry.

The older lesbian and her wife, both kind,
tell me *That's great,* assuming I mean invisible.

What I mean: men will call me any old slur
because surely one will stick.

—

On *Game of Thrones,* Theon Greyjoy's rape
is played for laughs, his cock cut off
and mailed for laughs. A man without

a cock should sleep with dogs,
might as well forget how his own name tastes.
When Missandei and Grey Worm had sex

I cried with headphones on,
assumed it approximated the sex I have,
which is not makeshift.

—

Men get their heads cracked open
with ball-peen hammers. What's not to like?,

my friend says, recommending *Never Really Here.*
It's true that I experience revenge fantasies

against men differently now, sympathize
and yet feel some knee-jerk fear, a shadow-self

that hovers and moves on.

They're nothing like you.

—

Who is like me?

A girl prayed *let me be sea*
and ended up a man. Who is like me?

Theon, after the cruelty foams away.
Before? What I know

spools like my boyfriend's hands
picking salt off my nipples. Who is like me?

My boyfriend says *dear* and sure, that's one heart.

TRANSIVERSARY

The further I get from being a woman waiting for T to melt my neck flesh already.

I know it's rude to be this ugly because in second grade my teacher said *It's not over till the fat lady sings* and a boy responded *Sing, Jennifer, Sing* to dole out the necessary punishment. Like how my classmates used my full name, mimicked me when I rocked back and forth (Jennifer, *don't be a freak / don't cry down your fat cheeks*), how rumor was I'd kissed a girl and this too made me worthless.

I dream a ghost called The Master belittles me in my too-small towel, but I'm never moved to shriek. I read liposuction forums, imagine my chin fat sucked through a blue-striped straw. In an alternate timeline, I go to high school naked but my body, recovered from dozens of surgeries, is fine, all fine.

Say Not Yet

Sometimes / pretend to be the last thing I need / which one of us is the man / (neither) / which one of us is good / (my tongue doesn't know) / Sometimes pretend you're rope / sometimes the hammer // there's a clearing / painting targets on our backs / with elm sap / (If we saw a visual of how trees talk / we'd never speak again) / Sometimes / be the last thing I need / say not yet / which is different than no // say boy you are the barnacle / wedded to the world / I will not fail / to dislodge you

Say / be the landscape / I'm chipping away / to surrender your center // Sometimes / be the last / I'll ever need / say not yet / your germs on my germs / (we'll never speak again)

INHERITANCE

I stayed an alcoholic when everyone
grew out of it. Orange top
means a smaller needle, an orange
sinking into beer. She stayed a woman
for drugstore highlighter, bourbon from
the Rite-Aid. We fell on the sidewalk,
bled in a claw-foot tub. I stayed
an alcoholic when everyone
grew out of it. She dyed her hair,
buzzed the sides of head, put her
tongue in their mouths to be polite.
Purple top means the needle
pulling testosterone from
the bottle. She stayed an alcoholic
through the first shot,
the rush when she fled, the days
after I stayed and called our name,
 hers bleeding into mine.

LILY-LIVERED

"It's okay, I don't even cry
all I think about is a memory
and the dream when you kissed my arm
as I look away, don't hear what I say"

—*Land of Talk*, "It's Okay"

In a shotglass with honey coating the rim,
I'm almost 30, looking back at myself.

My tongue presses against the glass.
I hate my pink hair, the feathers left of my lipstick

called Wolvesmouth—later this is what she'll think
I have, an aptitude for carnage. Later our memories

will feather, frosted from other, similar nights.

Frosted from other similar nights,
I've mimed *let me sleep* but turned over,

my rabbit-light his fingers so deep
I bleed on the sheets.

Sometimes she fed stray animals,
wearing a collar to signify what she'd deny now.

Now she'd pull out my creamy liver with her own hands,
drop it on the counter next to cherry coffee.

Drop it on the counter next to cherry coffee
push my back against the island

Let's pretend no one wants anyone
my flawless nylons balled up

your hand tight around my neck
(let's make this count because it doesn't)

Let's make this count because it doesn't;
we pose for a photo where I look

so fat I've untagged it forever.
I take this high-gloss lipstick and draw

the shape of a man curled into his womb,
grind the photo's dress into meal-worm slits.

We never knew who should lead at 80s nights;
we don't know who should erase us now.

We don't know who should erase me now.

She said she hoped I'd die like roadkill,
star-nosed and dropped where I began.

She'd dig her nails into my thigh
to cut me into stars. My liver's creamy

fresco, drying in the sun. My liver's
stomped lilies, whiskey

in her sweating glass.
She said I deserved a slice of glass

pressed into my thigh. *Break
where you've begun*, she said,

roadkill creaming in the sun.

Like roadkill, my pussy creams in the sun,
under the orange lights of the gay bar,

the cool metal table of *sexual history.*
My liver is the lily that won't wilt under glass

no matter how much I pour straight down

my throat to forget you, Wolvesmouth,
who am I showering off when I can't touch

my own stars I'm so sick with our stems.

My friend hears   voices the hiss

        of our records turning over

           I saw   *something I was not supposed to see*

My friend hears voices

        stack like sweet foods she won't touch

I become the double-stuff oreo falling

        from her crumb tower

Walking to the Red Hook pier the cherries of our cigars
ash twitched and fell into the condom-littered water

I become the plate of pits   a stem she twists while we sit on the couch

        I saw something I was not supposed to see

           the ghostly swell in me
           like a voice rising the steam off our skins
           When we're showering off who we're

showering off   *I was not supposed to*

My friend hears voices   the hiss

of a procession

I have to have a picture
in my head when I listen to an album
even if I don't want one

The scabs come loose from her fingers   fall into my waiting drink

Mistake me for the man she's seasoned

My friend hears voices   the hiss

                                                   of pretty baby

I returned for the flood   the stars singed across my hands

                         She mistook for the boy I was

snuck me to session-beer heaven

                                       to season my gums

I caress the contours of a typical ditch
to figure out how a body spills there

                                           the inches of water I might absorb

Caress the contours of a typical ditch

                        register of secrets pill-thick in my pockets

My friend hears voices   frosted from other, similar nights

      My friend hears voices   hiss

                      from the record we're both too drunk

star-nosed and dropped where we begin

She mistook me for the boy I was. Snuck me to session-beer heaven to season my gums. We cried in her car while the 80s music played. I took another shot, didn't leave when I could stay. I took another shot, didn't sigh when I could sweat. I took another shot, did she ask if I was wet? She mistook for me a boy she could slap. Stung my cheek with her hand and never looked back. She put her hands in my jeans; I remembered what I lacked. Pulled her hands off me, and we'll always look back. She says I hurt us, boy I was, and we'll always look back. Caress the ditch, drop the record, and we'll always look back.

CARESS THE CONTOURS OF THE DITCH

In the dream he   invites me for a tryst in the men's bathroom anyway
Holds the door open for me
        caress the contours of the ditch   my friend asks how I knew
        the voices were all mine
The door he opened led to diner seats
What kind of man are you when everyone   has been so nice
a transgender register   of secrets pill-thick
        caress the contours of the ditch   my friend asks how I knew
        he'd bend me over only in   the safety of my own mind
The door he opened led to a deep freezer
The door he opened led to a plate of fries   I fell in love with them
        Opened my mouth like a ditch
I ate them all he said   *Oh no, I need you closer*

Lily-Livered is the Inheritance

I want to tell her I'm sorry, that the knife becomes reddest
when possibility enters the field—again—dripping like horses
chewed by the moon until their fur gleams
with tartar. I want to tell her *sorry* became the knife—
pressed to my stubble, my stubble the possible field.
Please, a horse dies to make me what I am,
the foam on his muscles, the foam in my lungs remembers the moon
needs me watery, my liver watered. Please, I want to tell her, I'll stay
alive just enough, anchored by the bit in my mouth, drinking anyway,
drinking.

TRANSIVERSARY

The therapist is safe. The ground is safe. The dog mouthing my hand, spreading flecks of drool like a colonizing fungus, is safe, is safe. The best word that rhymes with safe is safe. Her hand stroking my hair back to wake me up safe. His hand stroking the waistband of my jeans safe. This subway car, empty of people, full of vape smoke and fry smell and crushed cans, is safe. Safe: dropped in the bottom of my glass, my legs stuck together like a little fly. I am the little fly, safe, the itch after you brush it away, safe. The ground is safe. This song I'll never hear in your voice, that's safe. The goose stalking me up to the pond shore is safe. It's not your fault, but I am safe. It's not your fault I am safe.

THEY HELD ME, THEY CHOSE ME
A CONVERSATION WITH
WREN HANKS & JERROD SCHWARZ

There are so many wonderful moments to investigate in *Lily-livered*, but I think it might be important to start with a broader discussion of chronology. This chapbook moves seamlessly through different moments in your life. Can you speak to your process of choosing those moments? What parts of your life did not make it, and why?

When I started writing the Transiversary series poems in particular, I was thinking about how I'd written about being a trans adult, but I'd never written about being an overweight, bullied autistic trans kid. Those experiences—of being perceived as an undesirable "girl," of being told my body was a problem to fix—shaped the eventual arc of my transition, and I wanted to honor them.

A few years ago, one of my best friends told me I "never looked away" when she was dealing intensely with a traumatic incident from her past. It made me think about how crucial the act of witness can be; the moments that made it into *Lily-livered* are the moments from my life I could no longer look away from, that I felt called to excavate and move past. The parts of my life I left out were the ones I felt could wait.

ature *Lily-livered* is intensely confessional, but with a greater focus on physical ramification than what readers might expect from the Confessional Poetry movement. What were some of the challenges in writing poems about the body? What were some of the joys?

Writing poems about the body as a trans person carries an extra responsibility because cis people often assume you're speaking for all trans people when you're only speaking for yourself! I've been told my body isn't complete or "whole" before and quizzed about the types of sex I'm "even able to have," which was the impetus for writing poems like "Legible" and "Barricades." So I would say my main challenge when writing about the body is knowing that, at least in some readers' minds, I'm representing a more universal trans experience and doing my best not to unintentionally speak for other trans and nonbinary people.

The joy of writing about the body, my body, is that it's started to feel like a home. I spent much of my pre-transition life dissociating when I had to engage with how I felt physically or what I looked like. It's such a relief to have *arrived* in my body, like a star fleet captain beamed up to their ship after being trapped in the mirror universe.

At *Driftwood*, we often receive messages from new poets asking how personal they can be in their poems, and I think this is an anxiety many new writers feel. Outside of steering them directly to this wonderful chapbook, what advice would you give to poets working with intimate material? What (if any) strategies did you use in *Lily-livered*?

Even if a poem draws from your own life, I think it's important to distinguish between yourself and the poem's speaker. The speaker of the poem has a job to do, and it's not the same job as if you were telling this same story at a party or on a friend's couch. In my opinion, the speaker exists to serve the poem's truth, not to relay every detail of a moment just as you remember them. The speaker can be brave where you were frozen, quiet where you were screaming at the sky. Finding this separation between myself and the "I" in some of these poems is what allowed me to dig deep without feeling so vulnerable I couldn't continue.

My favorite visual choice in this collection is the repeated use of the prose poem. What are the obstacles and advantages in using a form that can sometimes feel antithetical to other poetic goals? How did you decide on this visual format?

I love prose poems so much because you can make so much noise within a block of text; without the borders of line breaks, you can repeat and recontextualize endlessly. I love that you can hide couplets, a whole sonnet, in a prose poem, and because you're reading it like a paragraph you can read it very fast. I'm excited by the challenge of making sure readers know where to pause even without line breaks and white space.

I think I gravitated toward the prose poem in *Lily-livered* because I wanted the reader to be a bit suffocated, a bit underwater, during the moments I was representing. I needed the reader to be *in it*. I'm such a fan of prose poems that I think the only obstacle to writing one is when a particular poem doesn't want to be one! I think every poem has an organic and necessary shape; for some poems, prose is what allows them to sing.

Similarly, I wanted to draw attention to the repeated poem title "Transiversary" that serves as the backbone of the collection. While readers can guess the approximate timeline, there is a powerful tension in these titles that eludes specificity while simultaneously presenting poignant snapshots of your life. Were these poems ever titled differently? Was there ever any hesitation about focusing on this specific date?

These pieces were always titled "Transiversary," but in an earlier draft of this collection, "Transiversary" was one large poem with about twenty prose sections that were roughly chronological. The word "Transiversary" means different things to different trans and nonbinary people. For me, I'm specifically referencing the date I started testosterone, beginning my medical transition. It was important to me to focus on this particular anniversary because medical transition has radically changed how I've been perceived by others—people I love, people I interact with in passing, people who have hurt me or hold me responsible for causing harm. I don't think using another title (or different titles for each poem) was something that occurred to me when writing these pieces.

As an editor, one of my favorite ways to delve into a work is to study its word frequency. While there is not always a relationship between frequency and theme, I was fascinated that safe appeared almost twenty times in this chapbook. What is the significance of this word to you and your writing? Were there any words that stood out as more emblematic?

Safe is definitely the most emblematic word for both this chapbook and the period in my life the chapbook represents. Honestly, when I started this project in 2018, I was moving through my life in a panicked, terrified fog. Afraid of my body, afraid of my PTSD triggers, I listened to the song "It's Okay" by Land of

Talk almost every day. One of the song's lines is "your voice becomes my home." I had to make my own voice—these poems—my home. I've heard other writers talk about how the book they wrote "chose them." I cried through writing many of these poems, but they held me, they chose me.

I wouldn't be here without the ways my wife, my therapist, my family, and my other loved ones kept me safe in 2018 and beyond. I don't know how to exist as a trans person, even one with a good deal of privilege, without wondering whether I'm safe every time I'm out in public. I'm learning how to be desired without reaching for an escape hatch, but it's still difficult. Working in animal rescue, keeping dogs and cats and baby squirrels and grumpy boas safe, has helped ground me and keep me safe in turn. I wouldn't be here without the nonhuman animals who've touched my life either.

How long had you been working on this collection? What did your first-draft of the chapbook look like versus the final manuscript?

I started working on this collection in 2018 and submitted it for the first time in late 2019 / early 2020. I had both full-length and chapbook-length drafts of this collection in 2019. Initially, I thought of *Lily-livered* as a full-length so the first draft was much longer, but over time I pared it down to its final (and I believe stronger!) form.

Often times, you will hear authors make the contentious statement that they are moving on to new concerns in their writing. Are there any concerns in *Lily-livered* that you feel finished with or no longer care to write about? Inversely, what moments from this chapbook would you want to keep investigating?

I'm proud of how directly this chapbook deals with my life as a trans person and hope it resonates with other readers who have had similar experiences. At the same time, I'm ready to move away from the directly personal / confessional in my poetry, at least for a bit. It was painful to write about suicidal ideation, the accompanying substance abuse, and assault; I feel grateful for the closure these poems have provided me. It's like I closed an iron door or covered a path leading to dark, gnarled woods with orange leaves. I don't desire to return to the places these poems took me.

The connection between trans identity and the natural world, like the fish in "Barricades" who can change sex at will, is something I'm interested in investigating further, both in poetry and nonfiction.

More to that above point, what is next for Wren Hanks? Simply, what are you working on right now, and how might it differ from *Lily-livered*?

Right now I'm slowly working on a collection of essays about being a neuro-diverse person working in animal welfare. I'm moved by inter-species connection and relationships, but I also think the way we approach other animals can be arrogant and cause unintended harm. I'm interested in how my own boundaries and "communication issues" as an autistic person help me navigate these relationships.

I'm also working on a full-length poetry collection, tentatively titled *Reduce to Silence the Swallows*, about St. Francis that's focused on ecology and queerplatonic relationships. I have a complicated relationship to Catholicism (I went to Catholic school but never got confirmed / the church is rabidly anti-trans), but I admire St. Francis's holistic approach to loving the world and chose Francis as my middle name after I transitioned. I'm really enjoying doing a more research-based project—it's a nice change of pace!

What advice do you have for other poets? What are strategies, mantras, or bits of guidance that have helped in your journey as a poet?

My mentor in graduate school emphasized that having fallow periods was normal and helped you recharge. In the past, I've burnt myself out trying to be overly productive, chasing publications and deadlines so as to not get left behind. My biggest piece of advice is to lean into your fallow periods: rest, read the books you've been putting off starting, find a new passion or obsession that will fuel your poetry in the future.

As far as strategies, if I don't know where a particular poem is heading (which is often!), I tend to make it into a word game. Playing with rhyme and repetition is really generative for me, even if the final poem doesn't make use of either, so I'll start writing quatrains or use a refrain until I've got more words on the page to work with. This technique is how I ended with the prose poem in couplets at the end of *Lily-livered*'s title poem!

Where can readers find out more about your work?

Readers can find out more about my work at wrenhanks.com and on twitter @suitofscales. You can also purchase my previous chapbook, *The Rise of Genderqueer*, from brainmillpress.com directly!

Wren Hanks is the author of *Lily-livered* (*Driftwood Press*), winner of the Adrift Chapbook Contest, and *The Rise of Genderqueer* (*Brain Mill Press*). An alum of the Tin House Workshop and the Lambda Writer's Retreat for Emerging LGBTQ Voices, his recent writing appears in *Foglifter, No Tokens, RHINO, The Journal,* and elsewhere. He is the poetry editor for *smoke and mold,* and lives in Brooklyn, where he works in animal rights.

"Barricades" *DIAGRAM*, 2019.
"Inheritance" *Dusie*, 2020.
"Legible" *Indiana Review*, 2019.
"Transiversary [The further I get from being a woman I'm still not safe]" *New South*, 2019.
"Say Not Yet," "Lily-Livered is the Inheritance" *Periodicities*, 2020.
"Transiversary" [The therapist is safe] Third Coast, 2021.
"Transiversary [The further I get from being a woman the less I'm stared at while eating]," & "Transiversary [The further I get from being a woman waiting for T to melt my neck flesh]" *Waxwing*, 2018.

"Lily-Livered" takes language from the song "The Lament of Pretty Baby" by Cursive.

OTHER
DRIFTWOOD PRESS
TITLES

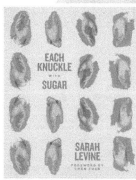

Printed in the USA
CPSIA information can be obtained
at www.ICGtesting.com
CBHW081740150524
8581CB00005B/57

9 781949 065107